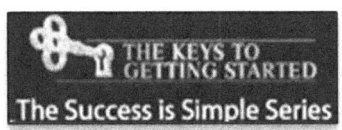

7 KEYS TO STARTING YOUR

OWN BUSINESS IN

7 DAYS FOR UNDER $700

Apostle, Dr. Jeremiah Thomas

"7 Keys to Starting Your Own Business in
7 Days for Under $700" v2

Book 1 in The Keys to Getting Started –
The Success is Simple Series
By
Keys to Life Coaching, Inc.

ISBN-9798868464874

DEDICATION

I humbly dedicate this book to my loving wife Kareen,
my children; Kalil, Kaitlyn, Elijah, Abigail, Tristan and
Elisabeth, and my dear sister Maureen, all of whom
I thank for continuing to show me patience,
understanding, and love beyond which
I could ever measure.

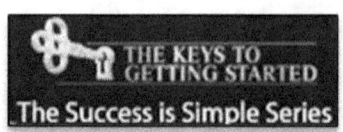

7 Keys to Starting Your Own Business in
7 Days for Under $700

Table of Contents

7 Keys to Starting Your Own Business in 7 Days for Under $700

Disclaimer
Important Legal Information

This book was designed and written for information, entertainment, and personal purposes only and does not constitute legal advice or an offer to sell, nor is it a solicitation to buy any security. The services, ideas, and information provided in this book are for personal, non-commercial, and theoretical use only. Potential business owners and investors are advised not to rely solely on any information contained in this book in the process of making any fully informed business decision.

All ideas, opinions, and/or forecasts, expressed or implied herein, information, charts, or examples contained in this book, are for information, entertainment, and personal purposes only and should not be construed as a recommendation to open, start, or invest in any business or investment. Any business ventures or investments made in light of the ideas, opinions, and/or forecasts expressed or implied herein are committed at your own risk, financial or otherwise.

Introduction

Have you ever thought about starting and running your own business? If you are like most people, you have thought or dreamed about starting a business and being your own boss. A 2023 Yahoo Finance survey found that almost 55% of all Americans desire to start their own business. For people under the age of 30, it's closer to 63%, and even 29% of people in their 60s want to go into business.

Yes, owning your own business is the American way. It is the basis of the

American Dream.

The ability and right to own your own business is a fundamental key to the pursuit of happiness and the underlying principle of the *Free Enterprise System* of the United States of America.

However, while so many people want to start a business and desire to be their own boss, less than 12% actually ever do so. The spirit of business, the spirit of entrepreneurship, has faded in the United States.

Years ago, the majority of people not only wanted to go into business but actually went into business for themselves in this country.

In the past, you owned a farm and raised livestock and sold eggs, greens, corn, and chickens. Or you operated a shoe store and resoled shoes and boots. Maybe your thing was a grocery store where you brought directly from the farmer and sold goods to the public.

People owned pubs, sold horseshoes and the business of undertaking was always a good investment.

Everyone grew up with the idea that you learned a craft when you were young, and you developed that specialty into your own business. That was the American way.

It is still like that in many other countries and even though it may be more difficult in some countries, the *spirit of entrepreneurship*, the spirit of business ownership still thrives.

I grew up in the Caribbean and my father owned a transportation company, and my grandfather owned and operated a successful farm.

I then came to America expecting the streets to be, *paved with gold*, as the saying went, but found that it was not all that easy to start your own business. Somehow, over the years, the mindset, the general way of thinking about career and business, had dramatically changed.

Today, the thought is to go to school, then go to school some more, and then if you are fortunate enough or have enough money, go to school even more. Then you go out and get a good job. That's it.

Most people grow up today with their parents and teachers telling them to prepare so that they can get a good job. Authority figures and those in positions of higher education, drill into the heads of everyone entering or about to enter the marketplace, to find a good job. This is the modern philosophy in America. The goal for most Americans is to get a good job, not to own a business.

Personally, I not only think that this is the most backward way of thinking I have ever heard of, but it is a way to develop a permanent underclass.

The people who *do* own the businesses and own the stores and restaurants, will always need people to work *for* them; so why not encourage more people to get a good job and go to work? Why not train people from childhood to work for someone else?

Don't misunderstand me. Owning and running a business is not for everyone. However, the option should be more readily available to *everyone* and that is the purpose of this book.

Upon arriving in the States and before I started my own businesses I looked up and noticed the *worker's mentality* that permeates our popular culture and I realized that for most people in this country, the mere thought of starting a business is unimaginable.

People feel that starting a business is a gigantic mountain that they could not climb even if they had the education and the money. They feel that starting a business takes...

✓ skill, which they do not have,

✓ the knowledge that they cannot get, and

✓ a whole lot of money which is out of the question.

The thought is, "Where am I supposed to get the money?"

Plus, let's face it; the economy isn't that great, the future is uncertain, and there are only so many hours in a day. All kinds of apparent valid reasons beseech the average person when it comes to starting a business:

"I have a job..."

"I have to keep my bills paid..."

"I have a family to care for..."

"I don't have the right education..."

"The timing isn't right..."

4

"The moon is not in the seventh house..."

"Jupiter is not aligned with Mars!"

Yes, making excuses for not going into business is part of the reason that so many fail to do so, but it is not the main culprit.

Most people look at the possibility of starting and owning their own business as an overwhelmingly intimidating, nearly insurmountable task.

Actually, those thoughts are correct; starting and owning your own business is indeed an intimidating and nearly insurmountable task. However, that is not the problem.

The problem is that the thinking called, "I can't do that..." has too many people trapped, captured, and imprisoned from trying.

Too many people are so blind to the *possibility* of owning their own business that they cannot even imagine such. They are so afraid of the thought, that they cannot even think it.

As we already know, if you cannot imagine it, you surely cannot do it. The mind must first be able to conceive the idea to begin to manifest it.

This way of thinking, of living in a state of fear and doubt, is not only bad for anyone and hampers happiness, but it is counter-scriptural. It is against the Word of God to live in fear and doubt.

As an apostle of the gospel of Jesus Christ, I cannot sit idly by and watch as people perish for such lack of knowledge. Since my life's philosophy is to…

teach them *how* to fish, rather than *give* them fish,

I decided to write this series of books.

Please don't misunderstand, this book is not about scripture or a bible lesson of any kind. It is also not a business school course. This book, written in plain and simple language, will help you see that going into business and doing your own thing is not as difficult as it seems, nor is it as expensive as you may have thought.

The Keys to Getting Started series contains several books about how to get up and get going. It will empower you to go forth, to seek out, and to capture your dreams.

For the purposes of this book, I am not Apostle Jeremiah Thomas; I am every person who has feared going into business and had limited finances to do so.

This book will help you to see that starting a business is very simple. This book will help you see that starting your own business is not only very simple, but YOU can do it and you can do it in less than one week!

7 Keys to Starting Your Own Business in 7 Days for Under $700 will take you step-by-step to getting started in your own business, right now, today. Whether you work full-time or whether you are retired; you can be in your own business by next week.

If you have a family that you are responsible for or if you are young, single and just starting your first job or college, you can be in your own business in just a few days.

Whether you have a nest egg of money you are looking to invest or have a mountain of bills and struggle to make ends meet every month, you can be running your own business for less than $700.

While I will at times refer to Holy Scripture, once again, this book is not a sermon or a Bible study. This book is also not a business school class or a class for continuing educational college credits.

The purpose of this book is to give you some very simple, practical steps to succeed where so many fail. This book will give you the keys; that is, the vital elements to starting your own business, in down-to-earth, everyday language and terms.

7 Keys to Starting Your Own Business in 7 Days for Under $700 will show you just how simple it is to start your business. No, starting a business is not the easiest thing to do, but it is quite simple. All you need do is follow some very basic steps, these 7 simple basic keys.

People who go into business are not usually any smarter than anyone else is; they just know the basic keys, the steps to achieving their objective. If you will follow the 7 simple keys in this book, follow these 7 steps, then you will be owning your own business in less than 7 days and you can do it for less than $700 total startup costs.

Now, does that mean you will suddenly own a thriving, multimillion-dollar corporation? No.

Does it mean that you will have a dozen employees who run around all day and do your work for you? No.

Does it mean that you will be able to sit back and watch the money come flowing in? Absolutely not. In fact, let me make one thing clear right now.

8

Allow me to straighten out one, often misunderstood concept of owning and operating a business.

Owning your own business does not mean that you do not work. In fact, it usually means you will do **more** work, at least in the beginning.

I know there are a lot of people who look at their boss and think, "He doesn't have to do anything except order us around..." or "All she does all day is sit back in that big office and tell everybody what to do. I wish I had her job."

If you have thoughts like those above, you are sadly mistaken. In most cases, your boss does twice as much work as you do. It may not be the same *type* of work, but he or she is working hard nonetheless. Of course, there is that rare occasion where you do have a boss or supervisor who skates by on as little effort as possible, but that is the exception.

If you are someone who wants to start a business because you don't want to work because you are just lazy, because you want to sit back and call the shots and make all the money without doing anything for it; then I beseech you to do us both a favor and close this book right now.

No, I am not going to give you your money back. Close this book and keep it. Put it in a closet or on a shelf somewhere because someday you will come to understand the value of this book and then you will read it and benefit from it.

Please understand that going into business and being your own boss does not mean *less* work. In fact, if you work, if you have a full or part-time job and you are going to have to start your business on a part-time basis, then the amount of time you invest in work is going to go through the proverbial roof.

As you finish this book and begin your own business next week, remember that you will work, and you will work hard. However, please note that while you will work hard, you will work like a business **owner** and not an **employee**.

Working FOR vs. Working WITH the Business

There is a big difference between working as an employee of a company or working as an owner of the company. Yes, you will work much smarter, but you will also work with a different mindset as an owner than one does as an employee.

Technically, depending on the business structure you set up, you may be an employee of your own company, but you will not work *for* your company, you will work *with* your company.

If you do not own the company, you are not a *part* of the company, then you have to work *for* the company. You are not connected to it; you are separate from it; you and it are not one and the same. Therefore, you work for the company.

On the other hand, if you own the company, then you are a part of the company and the company is a part of you. You are both in a sense, one and the same. Therefore, you do not work *for* it; you work *with* it, as it is you.

When you work with the company, as it is a part of you, an extension of who you are, there is a different mindset and attitude in how you approach everything that you do.

Now you are not just working for a paycheck, you are not just working because you *have* to work in order to pay the bills; now you work because it is yours, it is you, it is who and what you are.

Let me tell you a story, an analogy, a parable if you will, of the difference between working *for* and working *with*. It is the difference between an employee mindset and an owner mindset.

Three Men on a Construction Site

There were three men working on a construction site. They were deep down in the earth in an area that had been cleared and cemented over. The area appeared to be the beginning of what would be a huge room or parking area of some sort.

Each of the men was working in a corner of the great expanse, and each had with him a wheel-barrel full of bricks, a bucket of cement, and a trowel. It looked as though each was laying bricks in his respective corner.

A young woman came on the scene who appeared to be a reporter, as she carried a pen and pad in hand. She approached the first man she came to and said, "Excuse me Sir, do you mind if I ask you what it is that you are making here?"

The man maintained his brick-laying position on his knees, turned to look over his shoulder, and replied, "Yeah, I'm making $17.50 an hour."

The young journalist thanked him and proceeded to the second worker where she asked, "Excuse me Sir, do you mind if I ask you what it is that you are making here?"

This construction worker got to one knee, turned toward the reporter, and replied, "Why yes. I am making a corner. You see this is going to be a big room, one of the foundation rooms and I am making a corner of the room."

The reporter thanked him and moved on to the third construction man and again he asked, "Excuse me Sir, do you mind if I ask you what it is that you are making here?"

However, this bricklayer laid down his trowel. He stood to his feet. He turned to face the reporter, looking her directly in the eye. He then patted himself, creating a small cloud of white cement dust.

Filling his chest with air, he steadied himself and proudly announced, "Yes ma'am. I would be honored to explain the project that I am working on. You see, what I am making here is the future. Yes, I am making the future possible.

This is going to be a building, but not just any building. It is going to be the tallest building in this country! It is going to be so tall; I hear that they are going to put one of those beacon lights on top to warn passing aircraft!

This building is going to be a hub of activity and commerce; it's going to have a ton of businesses and restaurants, and stores. There will be offices throughout and luxury apartments on the upper floors.

Thousands of people will pass through here every single day and it will provide jobs for hundreds, even thousands of people in the community. It is the biggest economic boost to this county in history! This building holds the future of this community the future of our children!

And it is all possible because of me! This brick that I lay, supports the corner of the very foundation of the entire building.

Without this brick, the building cannot stand. Should I lay these bricks unevenly or off center, the entire structure will be off, indeed everything may fall apart! It is all my responsibility.

I am building the future, and I am the most important person in this project!"

Someone may be thinking that perhaps that third guy needs to decaffeinate. However, here is the question:

Were each of the three men doing the same job?

What do you think?

You see if you are like the first construction worker who replied that he was making $17.50 an hour, then you go to work simply to get a paycheck.

There is nothing wrong with that, but that is an *employee mentality*. That is a worker's way of thinking. In that case, you will always be working for $17.50 an hour, no matter how much an hour you make.

If you make upwards of $100,000 a year, you will still be working for $17.50 an hour and that is because you will always make a little less than you desire and you will always work *for* the company. You will always work *for* the money.

If you are like the second bricklayer, then you are building a proverbial corner. You are neither hot nor cold. You do your job and a little bit more IF it is in your best interest. You want to do your job, but only enough to build a little nest egg for you and your family and build a safe-haven, a corner for yourself. Again, there is nothing wrong with this, but it too, is a worker's mentality.

This worker will stay on that job, in most cases hating every minute of it, but as long as they can sock away a couple of dollars into the 401K, they will endure it. They will take whatever horrors the company dishes out until they retire, collect a gold watch, go home, and watch their big TV.

However, maybe you can see yourself as the third worker saw himself. Can you see that what you do, no matter how small or insignificant it may appear, is the most important task to the mission?

If you can see the future and see how what you do can help people and supply a demand, and deliver what people want and need, if you can see yourself being responsible for making sure people get what they pay for and get what they need, all the while ensuing a tremendous life for yourself, then you are ready to OWN. You are ready to be in business for yourself.

16

If you are ready to take responsibility and take charge and take control of your life, then come with me and follow these 7 keys, and in 7 days, you will be owning your own business that you will start for less than $700!

As I mentioned, getting started in your own business is simple. Here are the 7 simple keys you will discover:

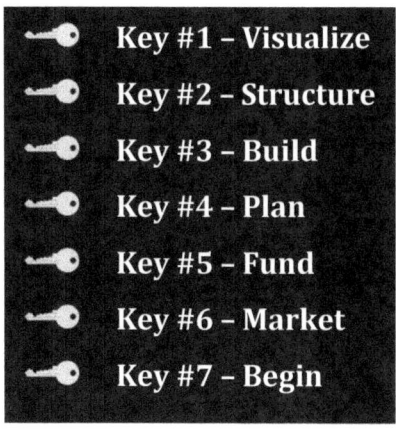

Key #1 – Visualize
Key #2 – Structure
Key #3 – Build
Key #4 – Plan
Key #5 – Fund
Key #6 – Market
Key #7 – Begin

Here is a quick overview before we get started.

Key #1 – Visualize: Visualize Your Business

You will learn how to successfully envision and imagine yourself in business for yourself. No, this is not about simply dreaming or wishful thinking. The fact is that you must be able to first conceive it and believe it before you can ever achieve it.

This step is the main key to accomplishing almost anything and the biggest stumbling block for most people.

We will briefly look at what type of business you want to start and expel some modern myths in the process. Finally, we will get into how to decide on what business structure you should choose and how to go about getting it done---today.

Key #2 – Structure: Decide Your Business Structure

In this section, we will cover how to decide what business structure you should have. That is, should you form a corporation, and if so, what type of corporation? Perhaps it should be a sole proprietorship.

We will examine your personal situation, needs, and plans, and I'll help you choose a business form and then direct you to exactly where you need to go to get the necessary paperwork to get started today.

Key #3 – Build: Build Your Business Relationships

Throughout your life, you have established many personal relationships. In business, you need to do the same thing.

I will show you how to create effective and strategic business relationships with such people as a banker, an accountant and an attorney. These are people you need in your corner. Don't worry...there is no money required!

Key #4 – Plan: Planning Your Business

Now, we will get into how to put the whole thing together.

I'll show you step-by-step how to take your ideas, thoughts, and dreams and create a successful business plan.

Not only will your business plan be your roadmap to running a successful business, but it will also be good enough to present to a bank, investor, or business partner. There is no business training or college education needed!

Key #5 – Fund: Funding Your Business

As the title of this book indicates, you will be able to start and fund your business for less than $700, and I will show you how and where you can even find that if you don't already have it.

However, you don't have to begin your business with only $700. Perhaps you feel that you will need several thousand dollars to start your dream business. Have no fear, because I will show you where to get it. Don't worry...there is no credit needed!

Key #6 – Marketing: Marketing Your Business

Now, you will learn some of the most exciting and effective ways to market your business with little or no money.

You will learn how the internet is the great equalizer. You will find ways to promote your business all over the world for pennies.

Key #7 – Begin: Begin Doing Business

Talk is cheap. Everything that you learn in this book is useless unless you get up and do something and this book will guide you to opening up and getting your first customers in the door.

There's nothing left now but to do it.
Are you ready?
Then let's go to work!

KEY #1: Visualize Your Business

"Whatever the mind can conceive and believe,
it can achieve."

---Napoleon Hill
"Think and Grow Rich"

Napoleon Hill penned that iconic adage back in 1937. However, long before this truth appeared in Napoleon Hill's bestselling book, *"Think and Grow Rich,"* the Lord told us this in the Bible.

21

Indeed, there are hundreds, perhaps thousands of scriptures that relate to believing and achieving and asking and receiving, but let me draw your attention to just one of those powerful verses for a moment.

"For as he thinketh in his heart, so is he"

---Proverbs 23:7a (KJV)

While this proverb has far more reaching and deeper meanings, let us just look at the surface portion. The verse makes it clear that what you think, you are. Or whatever you think becomes real. However, note that the proverb qualifies the thinking, *"...thinketh in his heart..."*

You can think with your brain, in your head, or you can think in your *heart*. *In your heart* is referring to a deep thinking, a *belief* that is part of you and who and what you are. Surely, if you cannot honestly, *in your heart*, believe that you can and will be in business for yourself, then it is certain that you will never be in business for yourself. If you cannot conceptualize yourself as a business owner, you will never be a business owner.

Whether you believe that you will be a business owner, or you do not believe you will be a business owner you are right either way. As Henry Ford said:

"Whether you think you can or you think you can't.
You're right."

---Henry Ford

The first key to starting your own business is that you must believe; you must be able to clearly see yourself in the position of, and actively owning and operating your own business.

Now I know that right now, many readers are thinking, "Of course I believe I'll be in business..." or "I've always believed I would be in business..." or, "Yes, I can see myself owning my own business..."

However, I urge you not to jump to conclusions on this question. Do not be too quick to answer, and do not take this lightly. The reason I have this as the #1 key to starting your business is that it is the most important key.

When I say that you must be able to clearly visualize yourself in your own business, I mean that you must be able to detail exactly what you are doing and how you are doing it. You must be able to do more than simply *imagine* yourself as a business owner. The vision has to be more than a passing fancy or a fleeting thought. It has to be more than a dream.

If you think that you can properly envision yourself as a business owner, or if you have not yet done so, here is a critical action step for you to take right now.

At the beginning of this book, I said that I would take you step-by-step to starting your own business in 7 days for less than $700, and here is one of those steps. Are you ready?

Get a pen and paper or move to your computer keyboard and prepare to go to work.

Exercise #1- Visualization

It is now approximately two months from today. It is a Monday morning, and you are just waking from a good night's sleep. I want you to describe your upcoming day in detail. Write down exactly what you do from the moment you arise until you are at the end of your workday. Write down what happens every hour, step by step. Here is a generic example:

6:00 AM   My alarm goes off, and I get out of bed, jump in the shower, and I am out of the door by 7:00 am.

7:00 AM   I am in my garage checking over my lawn mowing equipment. I make sure everything is clean and presentable.

I make sure there is enough gasoline in every engine. I check the lines on my hedge trimmers and check to make sure the mower blades are sharp and secure. I make sure all my supplies are in order, and I load my equipment onto the back of my pick-up truck.

7:30 AM   I go over my calendar of jobs for the day and map out my route, and I am off to my first customer.

7:50 AM   I arrive at my first client's home for my 8:00 job. This is one of my regular customers, so I don't need to speak to the homeowner, and I go right to work. I complete the job and painstakingly walk the area making sure I have cleaned all the dust and debris from the walks and driveway and look over the whole job. It's beautiful!

9:45 AM   I arrive at my second job. This is a new customer, so I knock on the door....

Do you get the idea?

Listen, my friends, this is not a game or an exercise in futility. This is a matter of fact. Please be diligent in this role play and think deeply about this. Visualize everything about your future workday or work evening.

Maybe you wake up and go to your regular full or part-time. That's fine. You can start your day from the very beginning, including your job, or start when you get off work and start your business.

Perhaps you are not yet sure of what type of business you want to start. Okay, let's take care of that right now. As we do this, let me first address a few *myths* about going into business.

Myths about Going into Business

You may have heard some sayings, some of which may have helped to motivate you toward going into business or that may have sought to prevent you from making a move. In either case, let's look at a few age-old adages as to whether they are true or false.

You've no doubt heard this one before...

"Find something that you love doing and you will never work another day in your life."

True or False

False. Doing something that you really love is great. But make no bones about it; when you go into your own business, there will be work.

Even something that you love to do, when you are in a situation where you *have* to do it, even when you don't feel like doing it, it will require some effort on your part. There will be times when you have to work and don't want to. There will be times when you have to buckle down and do what you know you need to do. And this is where the hard part comes in.

You see, as the owner, as the boss, no one can make you do what you need to do. If you want to just quit and take a nap, you can do it. No one will stop you.

It will require work, dedication, and discipline.

I say this because, too often, people go into business thinking it is going to be a way to lounge around and sit back. Then, when they find out there is some real work involved, they fold.

How about this one?

"You must be passionate about the business you choose."

False. This one has led many people astray. The thought that you must have a burning passion for the busyness you choose to go into. This is simply not true.

Yes, you want to consider starting a business in areas that you love; however, don't dismiss those things in which you are good at and can generate money.

You may have a passion for art and may love to paint. However, you may starve to death trying to open your own art studio or trying to make a living selling your paintings.

Although you love painting, you may work as a plumber. You may not love your job, but you have skills and years of experience in that area that were good enough for the company to hire you. For years, you've followed orders, and watched your boss make stupid mistakes and said to yourself that you could probably run the plumbing company better.

Why not start your own plumbing business? Whatever your job is, it is very possible that you can do it on your own.

28

"You have to be an expert, have many years of experience or a specialized degree or certificate in your chosen area of business."

False. How many businesses have you patronized where you felt that the people running it were certainly not the best at what they did? A doctor, a lawyer, a judge, or anyone in any field starts out somewhere, and it is never at the top of their field.

In fact, in every graduating class of doctors and lawyers, some come out at the top of the class, yet many just barely made it at the very bottom of the class.

According to a May 2022 report from the National Jurist, in 2021, 42% of people who took the bar exam to become a licensed attorney at law failed on their first attempt and had to take it over again. While a few states limit the number of times you can take the bar exam, in most states in America, you take and fail the exam an unlimited number of times. My point is you have to start somewhere.

If you have a talent, exploit it, use it, and develop it, and you will get better as you go. You will gain the experience you need while you build a business. You do not have to wait until you have 10 years of experience. Start today.

How about this golden oldie?

"Build a better mousetrap and the world will beat a path to your door."

This one goes hand-in-hand with...

"Find a need and fill it and you'll make Millions of dollars."

Both are absolutely true. If you see something that you believe can be done better, quicker, faster, then do it. If you believe you have a better way to cook and deliver pizza, do it. If you believe that you have a method to help homeowners better care for their lawns, do it. If you think you have a more efficient way of delivering newspapers, then don't just talk about it; do it! Now!

Here is something for you to keep in mind:

"When you come across that thing that frustrates you every day, that thing that makes you angry every all the time, that thing that constantly makes you want to swear; stop right there!

Instead of screaming, cussing, and slamming your fist on the table, figure out what it would take to stop that thing from driving you crazy. Figure out how you can fix it.

Then, package the idea and sell it, and you've got a multi-million-dollar business."

--- *Apostle Jeremiah Thomas*

There is one caveat: you must do it right now. When an idea comes to you, you had better believe that it only to you. Dozens, hundreds, maybe tens of thousands of other people got the same idea. Then, it is a race to see who does it first.

Perhaps you can envision yourself in business a little clearer now. Go ahead and pause, get a notepad, and figure out what type of business you want to run. Don't worry, this decision is not one you will carve in stone, you can change your mind later.

This exercise is not so much for you to figure out your future workday or to know the exact type of business that you will be operating. This is to help you see past your current situation. You have to imagine beyond the boundaries of where you are right now.

I can preach many a sermon on this one topic, but as I said in the beginning, this book is neither a bible study nor a business school course. I said I would present the 7 keys to getting started in plain and simple language.

The first key is to visualize yourself in business. You must be able to see yourself owning and operating your own business and *believe* it. You have to *think* that you can.

I Think I Can

You are probably familiar with the old children's story *"The Little Engine That Could."* You remember, "I think I can...I think I can..."

Well, there is a lot to be said for the stories and lessons we teach our children. The classic children's story by Watty Piper, first published in 1930, as elementary as it seems, is a perfect example of the power of positive thinking.

That little train, trying to get up the steep hill, all the while muttering, *"I think I can, I think I can..."* until he made it to the top, and the chant changed to, *"I thought I could, I thought I could."*

You may be thinking, "I wish he'd stop, I wish he'd stop..." However, please understand, my friends;

this is important. It is vital.

The inability to see beyond your current circumstances leads to the inability to set clear and effective goals, which leads to the inability to reach goals. Lack of proper vision is the primary reason so many people fail.

You must have a clear definiteness of purpose. If you do not have a clear purpose and direction, then you cannot possibly get to where you want to go.

You can never finish a race unless you know in which direction is the finish line.

Unless you can visualize beyond your current situation, then you can never have a clear purpose to get beyond that current situation.

You are where you are not because of money or the lack thereof. You are where you are not because of racism or sexism. You are where you are not because of where, when, or to whom you were born, nor are you where you are because of a lack of education or other circumstances.

You are where you are in life today because of how you think and have thought. You are where you are today because of what has gone into your mind. I tell you the truth; you are in the situation that you are today because that is how and where you were able to see yourself.

Where you are now is where you actually believe you should be. Deliberately or inadvertently, where you are is where you envisioned yourself to be.

If you truly want to start your own business, then start by seeing yourself in that business. Write down the details of your future business day. I'll close this chapter with a short poem by that author, Napoleon Hill.

"If you think you are beaten, you are.
If you think you dare not, you don't.
If you like to win, but you think you can't,
It is almost certain you won't.

If you think you'll lose, you've lost,

For out in the world we find,

Success begins with a person's will -

It's all in the state of MIND.

If you think you're outclassed, you are,

You've got to think high to rise,

You've got to be sure of yourself before

You can ever win a prize.

Life's battles don't always go

To the stronger or faster man,

But sooner or later, the man who wins

Is the man WHO THINKS HE CAN!"

— *Napoleon Hill*

Think and Grow Rich

Chapter Recap

Key #1: Visualize Your Business

Average Cost of Key #1 =	$ 0
Key #1 Allotted Time =	1 Day
Total Cost of Starting Your Business =	$ 0
Total Elapsed Time =	1 Day

KEY #2: Decide Your Business Structure

The business structure, form, or type of business you choose will have lasting implications on taxes, liability, how you pay yourself and others, and more. While you can change your business structure later, it is important to choose one that fits your company and planned growth.

First, I'll give you an overview of the most common business structures and then we will examine each closer to help you decide on which is best for your business. For each of the business structures, we will quickly cover:

37

   a. The basics of the business structure.

   b. Forming the business structure.

   c. A little tax information for the business structure.

   d. Some advantages and disadvantages.

Finally, I will direct you to where to go to get your business structure set up so you can get started right now.

The 4 most common business structures are:

1. A Sole Proprietorship
2. A Partnership
3. A (C) Corporation
4. A (S) Corporation

A Sole Proprietorship

A Sole Proprietorship is the simplest and most common structure people choose when going into business. A Sole Proprietorship is a business owned and operated by one individual person. The business owner and *proprietor* are one person, the same person. As a sole proprietor, you are the business, and the business is you.

As a sole proprietor (SP) you are solely entitled to all the profits from the business. Likewise, however, you are solely responsible for all the losses and all the liabilities.

Again, a SP is one individual who owns the business. While a husband and wife are considered to be "one," and may file a single joint tax return;

<u>a husband and wife cannot be a Sole Proprietorship</u>.

Only one spouse can be the proprietor, and the other can work for the SP. You will find that many couples choose this option, and there are some tax advantages to this as well.

Forming a Sole Proprietorship

You do not need any legal paperwork or need to take any formal action or legal steps to form a Sole Proprietorship. You can just go into business. You will use your own social security number as your Federal Employer Identification Number (EIN) whenever asked for one.

For instance, if you are an independent gardener like in our earlier example, you are automatically an SP, though you can change that designation if you wish. However, there may be a few licenses or permits that you may need, and these differ from state to state.

Typically, if you are going to run a home-based business and you are not going to charge your customers tax, the most you may need is a *general business operating license* or "privilege" license. In either case, they are no big deal; just fill out a simple form and pay a small fee.

If you operate a business that could possibly cause bodily harm, like a barber, a manicurist, a masseuse, or something similar; then you may need an *occupational license.*

If you are going to operate under a name other than your own, such as an assumed name or a legal business name, then you want to get a simple DBA (Doing Business As), also known in some states as a Fictitious Name or a Certificate of Assumed Name.

Then you can be Joe Jamison, DBA "Joe's Lawn Service," for example. You can open bank accounts and deposit checks made out to Joe's Lawn Service.

Any of these licenses or permits will range from $10 to $125, depending on the license and the state. In North Carolina, for example, a DBA costs just $26 at the time of this writing, and in New York, it was only $33.

Do not let any of those things discourage you. For most SPs, all you need to do is start your business. When you file your taxes, most of those other issues will come up as you file.

U.S. Small Business Administration

To find out what, if any, business licenses or permits you may need, visit the *U.S. Small Business Administration* at www.sba.gov and go to "State Licenses and Permits," and you can get the information you need for your state.

Taxes and the Sole Proprietorship

Remember, as a Sole Proprietor (SP) you and the business are one and the same, therefore, there is no need for a separate tax filing. Your income is the business income and vice versa. With that, you need only to file your standard 1040. You will need to use the 1040 long form, as there are a few forms you will need to add to your return.

With your 1040, you will need to complete and add a "Schedule C," which is essentially a *profit and loss statement* to determine how much profit you made from your business.

In addition, you must add a "Schedule SE." As an SP, you have no *withholding* from your paycheck, and the Schedule SE accounts for things like Social Security taxes.

Lastly, you may need to file a form 1040-ES, which is an estimated tax form that is for any tax that the other forms may have missed. Your state and local taxes are based on your bottom-line income from your 1040, so file those as you normally would.

Special Note

Keep this one thing in mind:

YOU MUST PAY YOUR TAXES!

When you go into business and begin to take profits from here, there, and anywhere, the tendency is to forget about taxes. After all, no one is taking any money out of your paycheck.

Do not make that crucial mistake.

The IRS will catch up with you.

Estimate your taxes and put them aside as you pay yourself. For example, take 20% of your income and put it in a separate savings account. Then, use the funds to pay your annual tax bill or quarterly tax bill.

If you estimate you will owe federal taxes in excess of $1,000, you should file your taxes quarterly. It is the same thing; you just estimate some of the income and use the same forms mentioned above.

Advantages of a Sole Proprietorship
- ✓ It is very simple and easy to start
- ✓ The startup costs are minimal; it's very inexpensive to start
- ✓ Filing taxes is easy, basically the same as you do now
- ✓ You have total control of the business

Disadvantages of a Sole Proprietorship
- ✓ It is harder to raise money, additional capital
- ✓ You are totally responsible for everything, all the work

- ✓ You are totally and personally liable for everything that happens in the name of the business
- ✓ Failed debt and other financial problems from the business attach to your personal name and credit

A Partnership

A Partnership is exactly what it sounds like. It is a business where two or more people own and operate the business as partners. Each partner contributes to the business and shares in the profits.

Each partner is also responsible for the liabilities and losses of the business. Couples can and often do form partnerships.

Although it is not legally mandatory, you should create a "Partnership Agreement" between all the partners that details such things as the decision-making process, each partner's responsibilities and duties, how to divide profits, and what happens in the event the business fails; (A Partnership Dissolution Agreement)

There are two basic Partnership types:

1. **General Partnership** – Where responsibilities, profits, management, and everything else are divided equally between the partners.

2. **Limited Partnership** – Where liability, responsibilities, and investment are divided up according to each individual partner. For example, one partner may have expertise in the operation of the business but have limited resources, while another may have a lot of money but not very much expertise in operations. In such a case, one may be more responsible for the money and the other for operations.

Forming a Partnership

To form a Partnership, simply choose a business name and register your partnership with your state. You can get this done at the same place: www.sba.gov and go to "Choose & Register Your Business."

Taxes and the Partnership

Unlike a Sole Proprietorship, since there is more than one person, you cannot use a social security number as your EIN (Employee Identification Number) to file your business taxes.

No problem, though; simply go to the IRS at www.IRS.gov and go to "Businesses/Small-Businesses & Self-Employed/Apply for an Employer Identification Number." There you can apply for your EIN and get it within minutes, and it costs you nothing. It is free.

You will need to file Form 1065 (U.S. Return of Partnership Income) for the business, as well as your own personal income taxes.

Advantages of a Partnership

✓ Easy and simple to start; not quite as simple as an SP, but easy nonetheless
✓ Can be set up to take advantage of each partner's individual skill set and assets
✓ By sharing financial resources and responsibilities, it is less burdensome if things go wrong, and easier to raise capital

Disadvantages of a Partnership

✓ While the partners share responsibility for liabilities, those full liabilities still fall to the partners

✓ Sharing profits with multiple partners can cause problems when it appears that some partners may not be *earning* their fair share

✓ With multiple cooks in the proverbial kitchen, there are bound to be disagreements, sometimes major ones

Special Note

You can greatly minimize all the above disadvantages of a partnership by having a solid *Partnership Agreement* in place. Think about the possible problems and disagreements that can come up over the course of time.

This may be more difficult than it sounds because usually, at the time of getting ready to go into business, everyone is lovey-dovey and happy and the joy of future success is in the air.

You think, "No way! We know each other and love each other too much for anything to go wrong." Take this general business advice:

"It is okay to hope for the best, but you must plan for the worst."

You can get some examples of partnership agreements anywhere online. Entrepreneur Magazine online has one that you can download or go to some place like www.rocketlawyer.com, or www.legal zoom.com, or just about any place they sell business forms.

A (C) Corporation

When people refer to a corporation, usually they are referring to a type "C" or subchapter "C" corporation. A C Corporation (C Corp) is an independent, legal entity unto itself, and shareholders own the entity.

The corporation itself is legally responsible for the liabilities, debts, and actions of the business, and not the shareholders.

You would be a shareholder in the corporation that you start, but the corporation is responsible for the liabilities. The C Corp can also keep some of the profits in the bank as operating capital or distribute them to the shareholders in the form of dividends.

Forming a (C) Corporation

Starting a corporation is more complex than an SP or a partnership, and the legalities differ widely from state to state. You will need to register the C Corp, and the name and you will need to fill out and register "Articles of Incorporation," which spell out the details as to how the business will operate. You will need to get forms for your state, so start with your state website. For instance, in New Jersey, go to www.NJ.gov, or in North Carolina, www.nc.gov.

While setting up the C Corp is a little more complex, the costs are still minimal. You can file the needed paperwork to incorporate (become a corporation) for as little as $50. It can cost as much as $1,000, but I'd say the average cost for most small businesses to incorporate is about $100(at the time of this writing).

Taxes and the C Corporation

Remember, a C Corp is a *separate entity, like a person,* and therefore must pay its own taxes, which the IRS bases on its profits. It will also pay state and local taxes. You will need your EIN and file an IRS form 1120 (U.S. Corporation Income Tax Return).

Advantages of a C Corp

✓ Liability is the big plus. The liabilities of the C Corp are not held against you, the shareholder, nor against your assets or your credit.

✓ You only pay taxes on the amount the C Corp pays you in salaries, bonuses, etc.

✓ Raising capital is much easier as you can simply sell "shares" in the corporation.

Disadvantages of a C Corp

✓ Setting up a C Corp is a little more complex and can be extremely complex depending on the nature and size of your venture.

✓ Adding to the complexity are the differences in corporate laws from state to state.

✓ In some cases, a corporation can be taxed twice, once when it declares a profit, and again when it pays dividends (shares of the profits) to shareholders.

An S Corporation

Most small businesses or individuals, when choosing to incorporate, start an S Corporation (S Corp). The primary difference between an S Corp and a C Corp is the avoidance of the above-mentioned double taxation. The profits and losses from the business *pass through* the S Corp to the individual. So, as an individual who owns an S Corp, in a sense you get some of the liability protection of a corporation, but you file taxes almost like a sole proprietor.

Forming an S Corp

Forming your S Corp is much like forming the C Corp, and you need to file articles of incorporation, plus you will need to fill out a short IRS form 2553, Election by A Small Business Corporation.

Taxes and the S Corp

Again, with the S Corp, profits and losses pass through the business to you, but check with your state on S Corp taxes, as they differ widely. For example, the states of New York and New Jersey tax the S Corp's profits as well as the individual's profits, just like a C Corp for state and local taxes.

Advantages of an S Corp

✓ Tax advantages – for example, as an employee of the S Corp, you can get a salary as well as be paid in "distributions" from the Corp, which are taxed at a lower rate.

✓ Since profits and losses pass through to you, you can write off some of the corporation's business losses on your personal tax return.

Disadvantages of an S Corp

✓ The tax advantages of the S Corp make it a magnet for people who want to cheat the IRS, therefore, operational guidelines are stricter. You must keep very detailed records.

✓ Also, you cannot get away with paying yourself an employee salary of $7.50 an hour, and then take a *distribution* of $100,000 to avoid taxes. You have to pay yourself market rates.

Chapter Recap

Key #2: Decide Your Business Structure

Average Cost of Key #2 =	$ 100
Key #2 Allotted Time =	1 Day
Total Cost of Starting Your Business =	$ 100
Total Elapsed Time =	2 Days

KEY #3: Build Your Business Relationships

To operate a successful business, you will need to work with many different people in many different industries. The mistake you must avoid is spending too much time with people who do not add to the success of your business.

There are *personal* relationships, and then there are *business* relationships, and you need to draw a distinct line between the two. Yes, you can have your friends, but you will need to keep most of your friends at arm's length from your business affairs. You have to create several business relationships or what are called *strategic alliances.*

54

The Butcher, the Baker, and the Candlestick Maker

In your field of business, there will be certain specific relationships with businesses and organizations that you will work with over time.

As an example, if you start a lawn care service, you may form a relationship with the local lawnmower parts and service shop. You might form a working relationship with the managers and owners of apartment complexes and homeowner's associations. These relationships will become clearer to you as you do business.

However, in the beginning, there are a few foundational relationships or strategic alliances that, if you do not already have, you want to create right away. You need to create a relationship with:

- ✓ An Attorney
- ✓ A Banker
- ✓ A Tax Accountant
- ✓ An Insurance Broker

Have no fear; creating relationships with the above people is far simpler than you may imagine. I am going to give you a formula to follow that will guide you to starting these relationships.

It is simple, very easy to remember, and requires no money and very little time.

You want to call or just walk into your local bank. This can be a bank where you already have an account or not. Perhaps you may choose a bank that you want to work with someday, one in which you can envision yourself with doing business. Call an insurance agent who deals with all types of insurance, including business coverage. Contact a tax accountant and an attorney.

Either just walk in or call and make an appointment. Go online and search business attorneys, for example, and find an attorney who will give you a short, free consultation.

Here is a basic idea of what to say.

I am calling ABC Business Attorneys:

In the case where you get a receptionist or screen, you might start with something along these lines:

"Yes, my name is Jeremiah Thomas. I'm launching a new business venture in here New York and I'm looking to form a relationship with a good law firm in this area. I'm wondering if I might be able to get on Attorney Name's calendar for a short conversation."

Once you reach the attorney...

"Yes, my name is Jeremiah Thomas. I'm launching a new business venture in here New York and I'm looking to form a relationship with a good law firm in this area. I'm wondering if I might meet and speak with you (or Attorney Name) for a few minutes to see if ABC could be the firm I might need to retain."

Whoa! Say almost the same exact thing for all of them.

"Yes, my name is Jeremiah Thomas. I am launching a new business venture in here in Texas and I'm looking to form a relationship with a good (accountant, banker, insurance broker) in this area. I'm wondering if I might meet and speak with you for a few minutes to see if ABC could be the (banker, broker) I might need to retain."

As simple as this sounds, it is extremely powerful and sophisticated. Also, it is as honest as you can get, and I would never advise anything less.

Okay, so maybe you don't have any money in the bank. Maybe you don't have good credit. Maybe you work full-time and are going to start a business part-time. So what?

You do not need to approach people like a little scared, whining loser, boasting that you have no money or experience.

You must *act as if.*

You must act as if you *are,*

until you become.

That is the goal of the first key. You must have a solid picture of you and your success. Visualize yourself, and then approach these people as if you have a million dollars in the bank, and soon you will!

There are some critical key points to this introduction statement above.

You must act as if

you are

until you become.

1. **New business:** Mention that you are starting a *new* business venture. This opens the thought that this may not be your first or only business.

2. **State the State:** You specifically want to mention the state in which you are going to do business. This projects the image that you may have other business concerns in other states. People who operate on a national or international level speak in terms of states. *"I'm launching a new business venture in New Jersey..."*

3. **Form a relationship:** Tell the truth; you want to form a relationship. However, this statement gives the impression that your goal is more than to just open an account. You want more than to just get your taxes done.

4. **A *good* firm in *this* area:** This again, indicates that you may have other relationships in other areas. It also motivates the person to want to prove that they are a *good* firm.

5. **I might need to retain:** This is huge! The phrase that you might want to *retain them* is talking their language and the language of successful business people. When you say may want to retain them, you are saying that you want to decide if they are the firm you may want to hire.

Okay, so you have the appointment, or you walked into the door right off the street; now, what do you do?

Here is a formula for you to use in your meetings that will make you look and sound professional as well as help you accomplish the mission. All you need to remember is that you want to have a TALK with these people. That's all, just have a TALK.

T.A.L.K.

       T = Tell

       A = Ask

       L = Learn

       K = Know

T = Tell

First, you simply want to tell them who you are and what you are doing. The key here is not to talk too much. Be honest, but less is better in this case. You want to introduce yourself and give a very brief idea of the business you are starting.

If posed with questions that you cannot answer, choose not to answer in this manner:

"Well, I would rather not get into that at this time..."

Please understand, my friends, this is normal. Business people know that there are trade secrets, proprietary information, patents, and all sorts of reasons why a good business professional is not going to divulge too much information to someone he or she just met. They are used to talking to people in a first meeting who are very elusive, even secretive.

The less information, the fewer specifics about your business that you explain, the more it looks like you know what you are talking about, even if it really is the opposite.

People who run their mouths constantly about all the things that they have and can do, and the money they have in the bank are usually the exact opposite, and most true professionals know this.

A = Ask

Now, ask some questions. Ask those questions that you are thinking about right now. As you read this book, jot down questions that come to mind. Also, you do not need too many questions. Once again, less is more. And you can let the person know that the main thing you wanted to do was to meet him or her to get a *feel* for the company.

L = Learn

Learn from the meeting. Take notes. A good thing to do is use questions from one firm and ask the other. In other words, let's say you met with an accountant who mentioned her firm will accept your QuickBooks files on a thumb drive to do your taxes. You might turn around and ask the banker, "What do you think about me turning over my entire QuickBooks files to an accountant on a thumb drive?"

K = Know

Now you want to know and let them know that everything you now know is good to know.

- ✓ "It's good to know that your firm handles the types of accounting services I need..."
- ✓ "It's good to know that I have a good law firm to turn to in the need of..."
- ✓ "It's good to know that your bank offers all of these additional services..."
- ✓ "It's good to know that I can get key-person insurance for a partner..."
- ✓ "It's good to know your bank. It's good to get to know your firm."
- ✓ "It's good to know *you*."

Then, thank them and show appreciation for his or her time, and get out of there. You will be surprised as to what lengths people will go to, to impress you, and when they do so, you should be impressed. Be impressed, and follow up later when you need the help.

Just like that, you will have established the beginnings of some very critical business relationships.

Chapter Recap

Key #3 – Build Your Business Relationships

Average Cost of Key #3 =	$ 0
<u>Key #3 Allotted Time =</u>	<u>1 Day</u>
Total Cost of Starting Your Business =	$ 100
Total Elapsed Time =	3 Days

KEY #4: Planning Your Business

"Where in the world am I going to get the money to start a business?"

People ask me this question most often. However, the answer, like everything else thus far, is far simpler than you may think.

Before you can figure out where to get the money to fund your business, you first need to answer the more important question:

How much money do you need?

First, you need to determine how much money you will need to get your business off the ground.

This cannot be a guess or some figure that is PFA (Plucked From Air). You must *know* what you need, why you need it, and what you are going to do with it.

Then, you need to know exactly how your business will run and how it will operate. Where are you going to get customers? You can't wait until you are in business to answer these questions. You must answer them before you begin, and you must have a plan to make it work. You need a business plan.

Your Business Plan

Many people think that a good business plan is only to give to a bank or investor or if you are going to start a large, complex corporation. However, everyone needs a business plan.

Your business plan is much more for your use and for your education and guidance than for anything else. Your business plan is your personal *road map to success.* If you are going to start your business part-time from your garage or are going to launch a multi-million-dollar corporation, you must have a good plan.

66

As you complete your business plan, it will help you determine how much money you need to start and how much you'll need going forward to operate.

There are a ton of places to help you get this done rather simply. You can download a business plan template or software or start a business plan online.

LivePlan.com  **LivePlan**

Liveplan.com (www.liveplan.com) is a great place to start. LivePlan will take you by the hand and lead you step-by-step to setting up a very well-structured business plan good enough to present to an investor.

Programs like this will ask you questions about your business, such as:

- ✓ "How much does your product cost to make?"
- ✓ "How much time does it take to make one of your products?"
- ✓ "How much does it cost you to service one client?"
- ✓ "How do you sell your product?"
- ✓ "How much does it cost to sell your product?"
- ✓ "How much do you sell your product for?"
- ✓ And much, much more.

These questions will help you figure out all the details you will need to run a successful business. It will force you to learn what you need to know before you get started. It will prevent a lot of the shock of, "Oh my gosh! I never thought of that..."

Go online and start right now! Online plans such as LivePlan run around $20 a month, and most of the time, there is a special for first-time users for 50% off. However, you can complete your plan in a couple of days. If for some reason you are not satisfied, after 60 days, they will refund your money.

Also, LivePlan will show you how to form your business and turn your ideas into a business. They will practically set up your financial paperwork for you; you simply fill in the blanks.

Your business plan needs to have a few basic foundational elements:

A. **Executive Summary**

This is a short, usually 1-page summary of your business. This is also vital for you to formulate this summary in your own mind. You might call this your *elevator pitch*. It is a way to describe your entire business in a minute or two. It's a good idea to write your Executive Summary when you have finished your plan. Even though it comes at the very beginning of the plan, you need to know the whole plan to put the summary together.

B. Business Description

This is a detailed description of what you do or sell.

C. Products and Services

A breakdown of all your products or services.

D. Sales and Marketing

Now, you need to explain how you are going to promote your business. How are you going to get clients, make sales, and grow your business?

E. Operations

How will your business operate? Who is in charge of what? If it is only you, ok. But how are you going to do it?

F. Financial Summary

Where and how will you invest the start-up money and everything else you need to operate? How much will it

7 Keys to Starting Your Own Business in 7 Days for Under $700

cost you to operate day to day? What do you project for a cash flow? What do you project in sales over the coming year?

Don't worry about this too much. You are writing this on paper, not in cement. It will make you think and help you figure things out. The plan will ask you very simple questions to help you arrive at the necessary answers.

Also, these questions are not as difficult or complex as they may seem. Just get online and answer the questions. If you cannot answer the questions, then you need to do some research and find those answers.

Create a good business plan and then follow that plan. Your business plan is your guide, your *blueprint to success.*

70

Chapter Recap

Key #4 – Planning Your Business

Average Cost of Key #4 =	$ 20
Key #4 Allotted Time =	2 Days
Total Cost of Starting Your Business =	$ 120
Total Elapsed Time =	5 Days

KEY #5: Funding Your Business

Okay, now that you have a good idea of how much money you need to get started, where are you going to get it? Below are several funding sources. Depending on how much you need and your personal situation, one of these will get you the funds you need to finance your start-up now!

Personal Funding (Bootstraps)

Yes, this funding source is exactly what it sounds like. You fund your business out of your pocket. If you are starting a small, perhaps home-based business and you work a full-time job, this may be your best option. Add a small amount every week or month to your household budget to invest in your business venture.

You also have funds that you may be able to tap into in your home in the form of a home equity loan. You might also get very low-cost loans from your life insurance or your retirement plan.

Loan from Family/Friends (Debt Financing)

Talking to friends and family is just one of the reasons why you need to be able to explain your business idea quickly and concisely in a positive way. You need the ability to explain and sell the concept and vision of your business in a short summary. If you explain it well, your personal enthusiasm for the idea will take care of the rest. Find people who believe in *you* and your vision and ask them to loan you the money.

You might also ask them to consider investing in your company.

Sell Stock in Your Company/Partner (Equity Financing)

Yes, you can sell shares in your own small business to raise the capital you need. The difference between a loan and selling stock or shares in your company is that you never have to pay the money for the stock/shares back.

A loan will have a specific repayment agreement. For instance, you borrow $5,000 from your generous aunt Betty, and you agree to pay her back $500 a month. In this case, the $500 is due regardless of how well your company does, unless there was some other prearranged stipulation.

On the other hand, you might sell 50% of the ownership in your company to your aunt Betty for $5,000. In this case, Betty becomes a partner.

As the business grows and becomes more valuable, Betty collects on her investment of $5,000 by sharing in the growth and success of the business. Perhaps a year later, the business in now worth $20,000. Betty would still own 50% or $10,000.

However, just as Betty shares in the growth of the business, she also shares in the losses of the company. In other words, her $5,000 investment could go down considerably and be worth a lot less in the future.

In either case, there is no due date on the money, aside from Betty wanting to cash out. You can find information on how to do this all over the internet. You might start with a simple web search of "How to sell stock in your own small business."

These few other places may provide good info also...

Investopedia.com or

rocketlawyer.com or

allbusiness.com

Crowdfunding

Crowdfunding has become the latest in financing trends and a great example of how the Internet has empowered the average person. In short, crowdfunding is where you go online, post your business idea, and invite millions of people to invest in it or to simply *give* you the money.

There are different models in as far as the way they work. With some, the receiver of the funds pays the investors in the form of products or some type of special services.

While with others, it's just like selling shares where investors receive an equity stake in your company.

With some, the business owner sets a target goal of funds to reach, and if they reach the goal, they get the money. If not, they get nothing.

Then there are some that work where the owner will get whatever funds they raise, no matter if they reach a target amount.

A few to check out are...

Kickstarter (www.kickstarter.com) and Indiegogo, Inc. (www.indiegogo.com) and Gofundme (www.gofundme.com)

Business Loan

If you are thinking that you may need platinum credit to go to a bank to get a small business loan, you are correct. However, banks are not the only institutions that lend money. There are tons of small business lenders who specialize in hard-to-finance cases.

Yes, their fees and rates are higher, but you can't have everything. Companies like Kabbage (www.kabbage.com), SnapCap (www.snapcap.com) and

OnDeck (www.ondeck.com) are a few.

Also, check out PayPal.

PayPal Working Capital

(www.paypal.com/us/webapps/workingcapital) offers a business loan program, and PayPal is an easy start for a business banking setup as well. Set up a business account with PayPal that you use, like a paperless business checking account, and it will give you a way to accept credit cards as well.

Grants and SBA Loans

There are some grants available, but they are not very easy to get. There are very strict guidelines and rules to even qualify, and then you have to be really on top of

SBA
U.S. Small Business Administration

the game with a business that must prove its beneficial value to the community or the country. Go to the Small Business Administration and go to Loans & Grants.

Angels

Angels are essentially regular people with boatloads of money who are willing to take a chance on a good idea.

There are basically no rules or regulations to how or what an angel can or will do or ask for, as it all depends on whatever arrangements the angel and the business owner come up with.

Typically, angels ask for a very large share of the business, often a controlling share such as over 51% of the company. If the thought of the TV show Shark Tank comes to mind, the answer is yes. Those sharks are angel investors.

Starting Your Business with an Investment of Less Than $500

It should be obvious now that to find a few hundred dollars to start a business is not very difficult and $500 is more than enough to get started in a plethora of businesses. You want to remember that the main thing you need is enough to **get started**; that is just enough to get up and running.

Yes, it would be nice to also have 6 months of operating capital in the bank to back you up, but just get started. If you do need more than $500, you can find it.

Important Note:

Don't make the mistake of investing too much money in inventory or products. You want to be in a situation where your customers pay you first before you buy anything.

As an example, let's say you want to start a business where you sell sweaters. For years, everyone has told you that you need to sell those great sweaters you knit and give away as gifts, so, one day, you decide to go into business.

Once you get an order in mind, you purchase the raw material, and then you go to work to knit beautiful sweaters.

Let us assume that it costs you $30 in material for a bundle that gives you enough to make four sweaters. You figure you can sell your sweaters for $50 each.

What you do not want to do is start your business with a ton of sweater material in anticipation of a lot of sales. Don't go out and buy $300 in material ahead of the orders. Also, do not make the sweaters or go into production based solely on someone's "word". **This is a business.**

When someone wants a sweater, you take his or her official order and get a payment. Get the money in *advance* or, at the very least, get a down payment. Your minimum down payment should be at least enough to cover your tangible costs or the better part of the *cost of goods sold* and some portion of your time.

So, in this case, with the sweaters only cost you about $7.50 each, not counting your time. You might charge a minimum of $10 a deposit on all orders. Better yet, charge 50% of the selling price or more --- upfront!

Then, you take the money that you receive from the customer and go buy the material and make the product.

In the beginning, you want to minimize the amount of money you put upfront out-of-pocket.

You want to use the customer's money (O.P.M. – Other People's Money) to fund your orders.

In fact, this is one way of funding your entire business. Let's say you need $2,000 to start your business. Take orders and down payments in advance. Once you get your $2,000, then launch. Be careful and be honest. Always deliver what you sell.

If you sell a product that is so customized that you will not be able to sell it to anyone else, then you may want a bare minimum of a 50% down payment or the whole thing paid in advance.

Look, if you bake this huge beautiful, world's-greatest birthday cake that says "Happy Birthday Lil' Johnny" all over it, and Lil Johnny's mom does not come through and pay for that cake, you will have to eat it...literally.

Not only will you be out of the money, but you are out of the time it took you to make that cake, and that is where your real value lies. When you were baking cakes as a nice neighbor, that was one thing. But this is business, and as a business, it's business. Period.

For the sake of clarity, I'll assume you fund your business by the bootstraps, or you borrow the $400.

Chapter Recap

Key #5 – Funding Your Business

Average Cost of Key #5 =	$ 400
<u>Key #5 Allotted Time =</u>	<u>1 Day</u>
Total Cost of Starting Your Business =	$ 520
Total Elapsed Time =	6 Days

KEY #6: Marketing Your Business

Now, it's up to you to get the word out about your business. You have to attract business, make sales, and find customers. In the next book in this *Keys to Getting Started* series, I will get deeper into marketing and sales strategy. For now, I will give you some quick basics to help you get started today.

I mentioned a little earlier that the internet has empowered the average person and nothing can be truer. You absolutely must have a solid presence on the internet.

There are a lot of ways to develop a strong and effective presence on the web, and some of them can be very costly and require some serious expertise. However, there are many steps that you can take that require little knowledge and skill and even less money.

A Website

The first place to start in building your internet presence is to get a decent website. You must have a website. I don't care if you sell widgets, have a lawn care service, do plumbing, cater weddings, or own a corner grocery store; get a website.

In this day and age, if you do not have a website, you do not exist. Your website is your basic listing, your modern "Yellow Pages" listing. Today, when people are looking for a business, any type of business, they do not generally turn to the telephone book.

They are going to pick up their smartphone, their iPad or get on a laptop or PC. When someone picks up that smartphone and commands, "Show me the nearest florist..." your flower shop needs to show up in the results of that search.

While building an effective website can require specialized skill and training, there are several places that give you all the basics. All you really need to do is fill in the blanks. A few to check out are:

Web.com (www.web.com),

GoDaddy (www.godaddy.com),

Weebly (www.weebly.com)

VistaPrint (www.vistaprint.com)

These websites give you templates that you can simply customize with your information to create a decent-looking website. They also will set you up with your own domain name/URL.

Choosing a Domain Name or URL

For the sake of simplicity, consider your domain name and your URL one and the same. Your domain name (URL) is your web address, not unlike the street address of your store.

It is the name of your website. For instance, GoDaddy's is www.godaddy.com. Be careful and strategic in choosing a domain name.

You have to remember that this name, this URL, is how people will be able to find your business on the internet. In finding you on the internet, people use "search engines" like Google, Yahoo, and MSN, etc.

So, you want a URL that will be easy for search engines to recognize.

The temptation will be to choose a name that says who you are or some fancy, cute title. For example, you own a florist shop and you specialize in beautiful floral arrangements. You may want a URL like Susan's Great Arrangements = www.susansgreatarrangements.com.

This is a serious and very common mistake. The problem is that people who are looking for a florist online are not going to type in "great arrangements" into a search engine.

If you needed to find a florist in your town, what would you enter? You would likely enter something like "florist," or "flowers," or "flowers and gifts," or something of the sort.

You want a domain name that is close to what people will enter into a search engine. Therefore, you might choose something more like www.susans**flowers**.com or www.susans**flowers**and**gifts**.com. Does that make sense?

You will pay for two separate items:

1. The domain name/URL
2. The website (web platform, tools and templets and hosting of the website)

On average, at the time of this writing, you are looking at about $10 to $15 for the domain name for one year. Many web design platforms will give you a free or greatly discounted domain name when you buy their website tools and hosting.

For the website, it's going to run about $100 to $150 a year. You can also pay monthly, ranging from about $10 to $25 a month.

To conserve money and get started, take a monthly contract, which you can cancel at any time. You'll pay a little more than the annual method, but it's not all that much.

YouTube Channel

Second, on your list for building a web presence is to create a YouTube Channel. Remember, this is about search engines, and believe it or not, YouTube is the second largest and second most-used search engine in the world after Google. It's actually a part of Google.

It is not very difficult to set up your own YouTube Channel and the benefits are enormous. You may not have enough money to create a commercial and get it on one of the major networks like ABC, NBC, or CNN, but you can create your own commercial video on your phone for your business and get it on the air on your own YouTube Channel.

All you need is a Google email address, a "Gmail" account. If you do not have one, just go to Google and sign up. It's easy, fast, and free.

Then, create a short, 2-to-3-minute video. Just have you or someone talking about your new business.

Then, upload the short video to YouTube. Don't worry about having a YouTube account. You will be creating your account as you go. Your YouTube channel is also free.

Then, take that video and put it on your website and on your Facebook page.

Facebook

If you do not yet have one, you should invest a little time in setting up a Facebook page. I know your first thought is that Facebook is a bunch of kids playing around. However, believe it or not, the average age of a Facebook user in the U.S. is around 34.

Get on Facebook and set up a "Likes" page, (commercial, business page) rather than a personal page. If you already have a personal Facebook page, that's great. You will set up your likes page from your personal page.

It's not very complicated; almost self-explanatory and you will find hundreds of short tutorials all over the place.

Post links to your website and YouTube channel on your Facebook page and make an announcement asking friends and family to check out and "like" your Facebook page.

Business Cards and Flyers

If you have the skills to design and print business cards on your laptop, then go ahead and get a package of blank cards and print 100 off on your own printer for about $5. If you are not able to do that, then once again, there are websites that make this extremely easy. Check out VistaPrint (www.vistaprint.com), Got Print (www.gotprint.net) and Overnight Prints (www.overnightprints.com)

These sites will allow you to virtually fill in the blanks and create professionally looking business cards.

Again, if you possess the skill set, then design and print a few flyers. If not, you can order these online as well. On average, get a small order of business cards for $15 and flyers for $25 to $50.

Chapter Recap

Key #6 – Marketing Your Business

Website Domain Name/URL:	$12
Website platform and hosting:	$15
YouTube Channel & videos:	$ 0
Facebook Likes Page:	$ 0
Business Cards:	$20
Flyers:	$20
Miscellaneous/not thought of:	$83
Total:	$150

Average Cost of Key #6 =	$ 150
Key #5 Allotted Time =	1 Day
Total Cost of Starting Your Business =	$ 670
Total Elapsed Time =	7 Days

KEY #7: Begin Your Business

There's nothing left to do now but to do it. The only way it happens, the only way anything happens, is if you make it happen. You have got to get up and go to work.

You have the keys that you need; now, you must take a step. Yes, the 7th and final key to starting your own business in 7 days for less than $700 is **action**.

I urge you to start right now. Do something; just one thing right now, and I mean this instant. Put this book down and do one of the action items in this book right now. Let's look at the keys to this point.

Key #1: Visualize Your Business

You first need to be able to close your eyes and see yourself in business.

You must visualize your business and your success. If you have not yet decided on a business or industry or you have not done the visualization exercise, do it right now. Visualize your day in your own business from the time you wake up until you go to bed. Visualize every step of a day in the life.

Key #2: Decide Your Business Structure

If you have not already done so, figure out what type of business you want to form right now. If it is to be a sole proprietorship, then get it done now. Go online and register a fictitious business name. Find the corporate documents you need to form your S Corporation or gather the paperwork you need for partnership agreements. Do it now.

Key #3: Build Your Business Relationships

Have you not yet contacted an attorney or an accountant? Do it now. Get online, choose one, and make a telephone call. Set up an appointment today.

Begin getting some strategic alliances in order. Remember, it is simple; you just want to have a *talk* with them:

> T = Tell
>
> A = Ask
>
> L = Learn
>
> K = Know

You want to TELL them who you are and give a brief explanation of what you are doing. Then, ASK some questions. Get some good information. LEARN from what you hear. Take notes. Then, finally, let them know that what you have learned is good for you to KNOW. Remember, don't overdo it! Less is more.

Key #4: Planning Your Business

Have you begun your business plan yet? What are you waiting for?

I know you have heard people tell you, "Nah...a business plan isn't necessary..." as they went back to their jobs. A business plan is essential to your success. Check out Live Plan or something, just get it done.

When you fail to plan, you plan to fail

Remember, your business plan is more than something to use to try to raise money. It is your own personal guide.

Doing a business plan will force you to ask yourself tough questions about your business, questions that you probably have not thought of before.

Key #5: Funding Your Business

As you now know, there is a ton of money available to you. In fact, you probably have more than enough money yourself to get started.

Remember, use as much of other people's money as you can. Collect on orders first before you put out money. Even if you start part-time, you can put a little bit of money aside every week, every month, as you go.

Get a low-cost loan from your IRA or 401K. Take out a small second mortgage on your home or sell shares in your vision. You can also go the crowdfunding route. It doesn't cost anything to put up a GoFundMe page. Just get started.

Also, remember not to take too much money out of your pocket up front for inventory. Your orders should take care of your *cost of goods sold*. This goes for almost any type of business you run. You want to purchase your merchandise or buy your materials based solely on confirmed purchase orders from customers with down payments.

If your friends cannot understand that as a business owner, you need to charge them upfront for some of the work you are going to do for them, then they can still be your friends, but you might want to think twice about having them as your customers.

Key #6: Marketing Your Business

With the internet, you can look as big and as wealthy as any other business. Build a website, set up a YouTube Channel, and start a Facebook page. Like it or not, social media is a marketing avenue that you, nor anyone else on this planet, can ignore.

The internet is the new telephone book and the new word-of-mouth. People say that they would rather advertise by word-of-mouth because it is the best form of advertising.

While there is some truth to that, the fact is that people do not conduct word-of-mouth the same way anymore. Today, people are still talking to each other, but they are doing less talking to each other face to face.

Today, word-of-mouth is via text messages, Tweets, and Facebook posts. Yes, they are still talking to each other, still spreading word-of-mouth, only now by electronic means.

If you are not in that arena, then you cannot even take advantage of word-of-mouth. You must build an online presence.

In the next book in this *Keys to Getting Started* series, I will get much deeper into how to market your business. I'll show you many additional methods to spread the word about your business all over the world if needed, and for little or no money. However, you start by getting a decent website. Do it today.

Key #7: Begin Doing Business

Talk is cheap. You must **do** something. Let me leave you with another story that may help you get started. It's a story eloquently told by legendary sales trainer and motivational speaker, John Landrine.

It's the story about Ol' Joe.

The Story of Ol' Joe

We are back in the mid-1970s in Atlantic City, New Jersey, where the state just passed the bill to allow casino gambling, and big casino hotels started springing up like wildflowers. With all their sparkle and glitter, the rest of the city survived in harsh, impoverished conditions, with thousands living in squander, often within sight of the glamorous hotels.

Ol' Joe was one of those less fortunate citizens who lived on the street. His home was an alley behind a small diner. The owner of the diner was a kind old man who often gave Ol' Joe some leftovers from his little restaurant.

One day, as Ol' Joe roamed the streets, he had to go to the restroom, and although he was down on his luck, as they say, he had his dignity and would not do such a thing out on the street. Besides, what he needed to do was a Number 2.

He looked up and saw one of those beautiful hotel-casinos just ahead, and he went in. He looked around and spotting the men's room, put his head down and rushed through the crowd of patrons as fast as he could. He knew he looked shabby and smelled bad.

He made it to the bathroom and quickly ducked inside, but when he got to a stall, he noticed there was a little machine on the door that said, "Deposit 5 cents please."

Some of you may remember pay toilets as they were very popular for a time. Anyway, Ol' Joe didn't have a nickel, so he walked back out of the restroom and saw a nice, finely dressed young man standing at the entrance to the Ladies' Room, no doubt waiting for his female companion.

Ol' Joe went over to the gentleman, and squeezing his knees together and trembling, he said, "Ah, excuse me Sir. Uhm, you see...I need to use the restroom, and I, uh..."

Well, the young man took one look at Joe and knew what the story was and he gladly gave Ol' Joe a nickel. Ol' Joe thanked him very much and ran back to the stall.

Just as he went to drop in the coin, the door opened and another fine-dressed young man came out and he held the door for Ol' Joe. Joe thanked him, but then he hesitated. He hesitated because he knew that the seat was still warm.

However, he looked past his fear and stepped in. He pushed really hard and used all of the tools that were available to him in there and he attained complete and full satisfaction.

When he came out, he immediately began looking for the man who gave him the nickel. Ol' Joe was going to give the coin back. That's the kind of man he was. He looked everywhere in the casino to no avail.

Then, he figured that the young man would have probably spent that nickel in the casino. So, Ol' Joe thought he'd leave the nickel where it belonged and as he headed toward the exit, he dropped the coin in a nickel slot machine, pulled the lever, and started walking out the door.

Bing! Bing! Bing! Bells went off! He had hit the jackpot! $68.55! Ol' Joe said, "Wow. What do ya' think about that?"

Ol' Joe cashed in his winnings, but he got one 50-cent piece, still insisting he would leave some of that money where it belonged.

He found a 50-cent machine as he was near the door, dropped in the coin, pulled the lever, and started walking away.

Bing! Bing! Bing! Bells went off! He had hit the jackpot! $597.50! Ol' Joe said, "Well, I think I'll try that one mo' again!"

He cashed in and got one silver dollar, went over to a dollar machine, dropped it in, pulled the lever, started walking away, and once again... Bing! Bing! Bing! Bells went off! He had hit the jackpot! $3,148!

Ol' Joe said, "Well, Hey! This is my lucky day! I'm not gonna stop now!" He took his winnings to the race track, where he hit 9 winners, two Daily Doubles, and a Trifecta.

He went back to the casino and played Blackjack, Roulette, and Craps all night. Before it was over, Ol' Joe had amassed a small fortune of $656,789.38!

Now, Ol' Joe did not blow that money, no, no. He was smart. After paying his fair share of taxes, he invested in a small restaurant. Yes, you guessed it; Ol' Joe bought the small diner from that old man who used to give him food. Ol' Joe bought the place and paid the man enough for him to have a great retirement.

Then, he hesitated, as he knew the restaurant business could be tough. But he looked past his fear, pushed hard, used all the tools and advice he could get and before you know it, he opened a second diner.

He worked hard, used all the tools and advice available to him, and opened a third diner. Before it was over, Ol' Joe had built an empire of over 400 restaurants and diners across the United States of America and a dozen abroad.

He was walking down the streets of New York City, NY one day and a young reporter was interviewing him and Ol' Joe had told the journalist how he got started.

Absolutely flabbergasted by the story, the reporter said, "My word, Ol' Joe! That is an incredible story! I mean, all of this, your entire fortune all from one nickel." He said.

"I bet you must wonder every day; you must think every day and would probably give your whole fortune to find out the whereabouts of that man who gave you that nickel."

Ol' Joe, in a top hat and puffing on a big fat cigar, quickly answered, "No. Actually, I never thought twice about him."

"What!?" The journalist objected. "But that's what got everything started. I don't understand…"

Ol' Joe, stopped and turned to the man and said, "I'll tell what I do think about. I'll tell you what I have thought about every single day since the fateful moment.

I'll tell you what I would wager my entire fortune to find...and that is the whereabouts of the man who held open that door."

Ol' Joe explained, "You see young fella; the nickel was insignificant. With all those old, dirty army jackets and fatigues I had on, I bet if I had searched through my clothes, I probably would have found a nickel on me.

I had a ton of nickels before that moment and I would have had a ton of nickels after that moment. The nickel was not the issue. We all have a nickel.

However, by that man holding open that door at that exact moment in time, allowed me to use that nickel for its greater purpose. Holding open that door, presented the opportunity for me to invest that nickel for a much greater return."

Ol' Joe concluded, "You see young man, the greatest focal point in your life will be when preparedness and opportunity meet at the same moment in time."

You Have a Nickel

I told you that long story to tell you this: You already have a nickel. By that, I mean that you already possess everything you need to start your business.

You do not need a million dollars. You do not need an Ivy League education or all sorts of degrees. Everything that you need, you already have.

God has endowed you with gifts and skills that will take you where you need to go. You will refine and strengthen those gifts, but they are already within you.

God already prepared you. He prepared all of us. He prepared you to live life to its fullest. He prepared you for success and prosperity. He prepared you for happiness.

Hopefully, this book has shown you an open door. The door is open. You should now be able to see that the door is open to a world of opportunity and possibilities.

What you must not do now is hesitate.

DO NOT WAVER.

You must look past your fear and doubt and take a step forward. Get in, push hard, use the tools and advice available to you, and you too will achieve complete and full satisfaction.

I thank you for your time and attention and I will see you in the next book in the *Keys to Getting Started* series!

Sincerely,

Apostle, Dr. Jeremiah Thomas

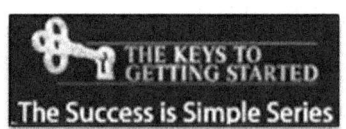

www.ingramcontent.com/pod-product-compliance
Lightning Source LLC
Chambersburg PA
CBHW072326290526
45794CB00002B/756